D1465488

700018688695

MAMMA MIA!
VOCAL SELECTIONS

MAMMA
MIA!

WISE PUBLICATIONS
LONDON / NEW YORK / SYDNEY / PARIS / COPENHAGEN / MADRID

EXCLUSIVE DISTRIBUTORS:
MUSIC SALES LIMITED
8/9 FRITH STREET, LONDON W1V 5TZ, ENGLAND.
MUSIC SALES PTY LIMITED
120 ROTHSCHILD AVENUE, ROSEBERY, NSW 2018, AUSTRALIA.

ORDER NO.AM959464
ISBN 0-7119-7454-3
THIS BOOK © COPYRIGHT 1999 BY WISE PUBLICATIONS.
www.internetmusicshop.com

COVER LOGO TYPE BY COURTESY OF McCABES.
PHOTOGRAPHS BY COURTESY OF PETER THOMPSON ASSOCIATES.

PRINTED IN THE UNITED KINGDOM BY
CALIGRAVING LIMITED, THETFORD, NORFOLK.

YOUR GUARANTEE OF QUALITY:
AS PUBLISHERS, WE STRIVE TO PRODUCE EVERY BOOK
TO THE HIGHEST COMMERCIAL STANDARDS.
WHILST ENDEAVOURING TO RETAIN THE RUNNING ORDER
OF THE SONGS AS THEY APPEAR IN THE MUSICAL, THE BOOK
HAS BEEN CAREFULLY DESIGNED TO MINIMISE AWKWARD
PAGE TURNS AND TO MAKE PLAYING FROM IT A REAL PLEASURE.
PARTICULAR CARE HAS BEEN GIVEN TO SPECIFYING ACID-FREE,
NEUTRAL-SIZED PAPER MADE FROM PULPS WHICH HAVE NOT
BEEN ELEMENTAL CHLORINE BLEACHED. THIS PULP IS FROM
FARMED SUSTAINABLE FORESTS AND WAS PRODUCED
WITH SPECIAL REGARD FOR THE ENVIRONMENT.
THROUGHOUT, THE PRINTING AND BINDING HAVE BEEN
PLANNED TO ENSURE A STURDY, ATTRACTIVE PUBLICATION
WHICH SHOULD GIVE YEARS OF ENJOYMENT.
IF YOUR COPY FAILS TO MEET OUR HIGH STANDARDS,
PLEASE INFORM US AND WE WILL GLADLY REPLACE IT.

MUSIC SALES' COMPLETE CATALOGUE DESCRIBES THOUSANDS OF
TITLES AND IS AVAILABLE IN FULL COLOUR SECTIONS BY SUBJECT,
DIRECT FROM MUSIC SALES LIMITED. PLEASE STATE YOUR AREAS
OF INTEREST AND SEND A CHEQUE / POSTAL ORDER FOR £1.50
FOR POSTAGE TO: MUSIC SALES LIMITED, NEWMARKET ROAD,
BURY ST. EDMUNDS, SUFFOLK IP33 3YB.

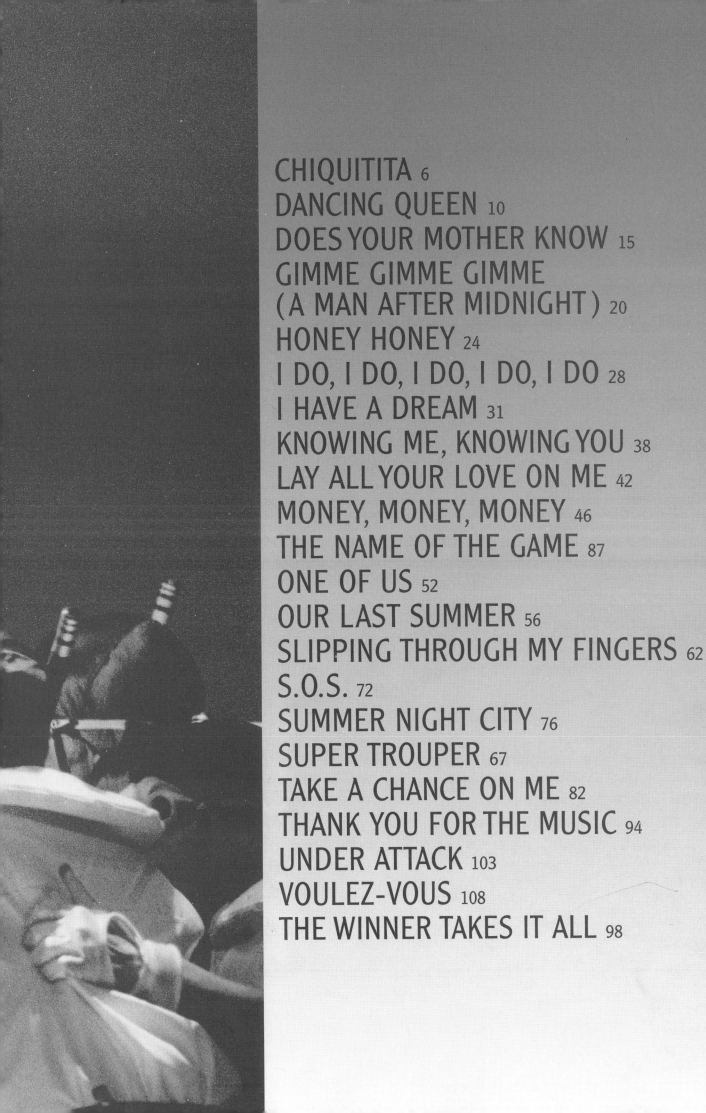

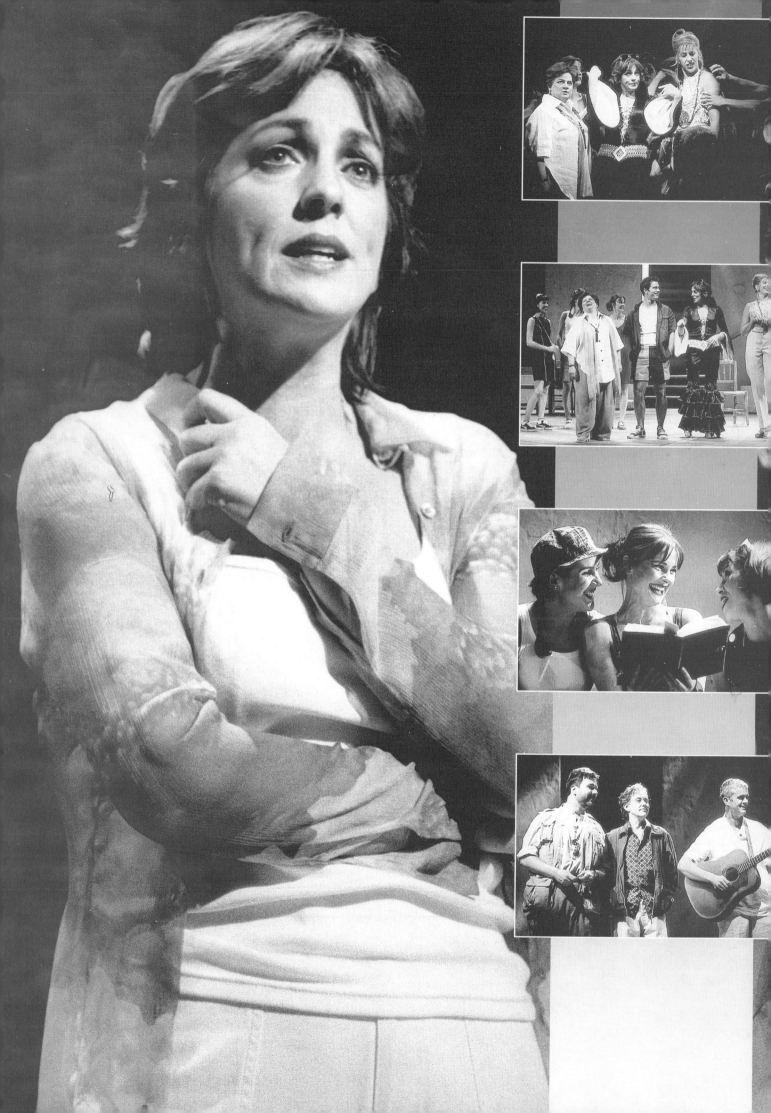

CHIQUITITA
WORDS & MUSIC BY BENNY ANDERSSON & BJÖRN ULVAEUS

DANCING QUEEN

WORDS & MUSIC BY BENNY ANDERSSON, BJÖRN ULVAEUS & STIG ANDERSON

2. A-ny-bo-dy could be that guy,____
3. You're a tea-ser, you turn 'em on,____

night is young and the mu-sic's high,
leave 'em burn-ing and then you're gone,

with a bit__ of rock mu-sic ev-'ry-thing__ is fine.
look-ing out__ for an-oth-er, a-ny-one__ will do.

You're in the

mood for a dance,_ and when you get the__ chance,_____

life.___ Oh,_____ see that_ girl,__ watch that_ scene,_ dig in the dan - cing_ queen.

repeat and fade

Dig in the dan - cing queen.

14

DOES YOUR MOTHER KNOW

WORDS & MUSIC BY BENNY ANDERSSON & BJÖRN ULVAEUS

8va optional

1. You're so hot___ teas-ing me___ so you're blue,___ but I can't take a
2. I can see___ what you want___ but you seem___ pret-ty young to be

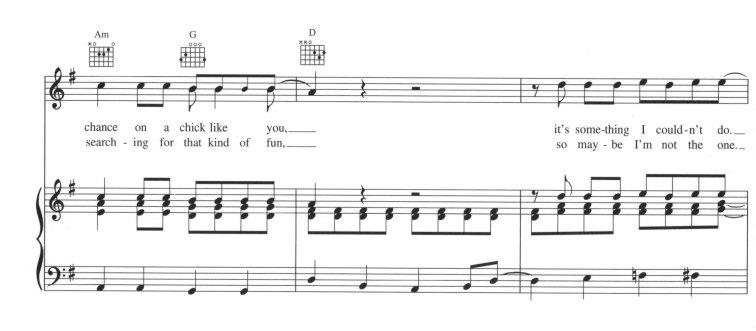

chance on a chick like you,___ it's some-thing I could-n't do.
search - ing for that kind of fun,___ so may - be I'm not the one.___

There's that look___ I
You're so cute,___ I

in your eyes,_ I can read_____ in your face that your feel - ings are driv-ing you wild,_
like your style,_ and I know_____ what you mean when you give me a flash of that smile,

ah,_____ but girl, you're on - ly a child._____
ah,_____ but girl, you're on - ly a child._____

Well, I could dance with you, ho - ney, if_____ you think it's fun - ny, does_

nice and slow__ (does your mo-ther know?). mo-ther know?).

Well, I could dance with you, ho-ney, if____ you think it's fun-ny, does__

8va optional

__ your mo-ther know that you're out?____ And I could chat with you, ba-by, flirt__

__ a lit-tle may-be, does____ your mo-ther know that you're out?____ Well, I could

repeat and fade

GIMME GIMME GIMME
(A MAN AFTER MIDNIGHT)

WORDS & MUSIC BY BENNY ANDERSSON & BJÖRN ULVAEUS

HONEY HONEY

WORDS & MUSIC BY BENNY ANDERSSON, BJÖRN ULVAEUS & STIG ANDERSON

Ho-ney, ho-ney, how__ you thrill me, a - ha, ho-ney, ho-ney.
Ho-ney, ho-ney, let___ me feel_ it, a - ha, ho-ney, ho-ney.
Ho-ney, ho-ney, touch__ me ba - by, a - ha, ho-ney, ho-ney.

Ho-ney, ho-ney, near - ly kill__ me, a - ha, ho-ney, ho-ney.
Ho-ney, ho-ney, don't__ con - ceal_ it, a - ha, ho-ney, ho-ney.
Ho-ney, ho-ney, hold__ me ba - by, a - ha, ho-ney, ho-ney.

I'd
The
You

don't wan-na see___ you cry,___ So stay on the ground girl, you

bet-ter not get too high.___ But I'm gon-na stick to___ you___

___ boy,___ you'll ne-ver get rid of me,_____ There's no oth-er place in this

world where I ra - ther would be._____

D.§ al Coda
to Coda ⊕

CODA

Ho-ney, ho-ney, how__ you thrill me, a - ha, ho-ney, ho-ney.
Ho-ney, ho-ney, let__ me feel__ it, a - ha, ho-ney, ho-ney.

Ho-ney, ho-ney, near - ly kill__ me, a - ha, ho-ney, ho-ney. I'd
Ho-ney, ho-ney, don't con - ceal__ it, a - ha, ho-ney, ho-ney. The

heard a-bout you__ be - fore,_____ I want-ed to know some more,_____ And
way that you kiss good-night,_____ the way that you hold me tight,_____ I

now I know what they mean,_____ you're a love ma - chine.__ Oh, you make me diz - zy.
feel like I wan - na sing,_____ when you do your thing,__ yeah.

repeat and fade out ending

27

I DO, I DO, I DO, I DO, I DO

WORDS & MUSIC BY BENNY ANDERSSON, BJÖRN ULVAEUS & STIG ANDERSON

1. Love me or leave me, make your
2. Let's get to-ge - ther, ev - 'ry

choice but be - lieve me, I love you, I do, I do, I do, I do, I
day will be bet - ter, I love you, I do, I do, I do, I do, I

found you at last. So come on now let's try_____ it, I love
just wait and see. So come on now let's try_____ it, I love

you, can't de-ny_____ it_____ 'cos it's true,_____ I do, I do, I do, I do, I

do._____

I HAVE A DREAM

WORDS & MUSIC BY BENNY ANDERSSON & BJÖRN ULVAEUS

Easy ballad-style

I have a dream, a song to sing to help me

cope   with an - y - thing.   If you see the

won - der   of a fai - ry tale,   you can take the

fu - ture   ev - en if you fail.   I be-lieve in

To Coda ⊕

an - gels,   some-thing good in ev - ery-thing I see,   I be-lieve in

dream,   I'll cross   the   stream,   I   have   a

dream, na   na   na   na . .

repeat and fade

37

KNOWING ME, KNOWING YOU

WORDS & MUSIC BY BENNY ANDERSSON, BJÖRN ULVAEUS & STIG ANDERSON

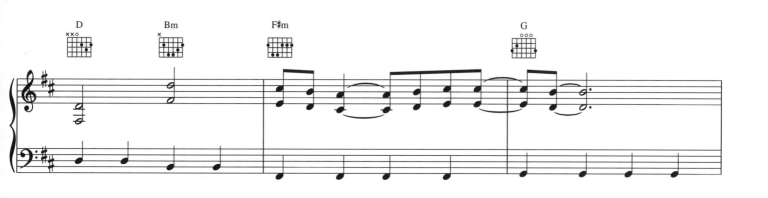

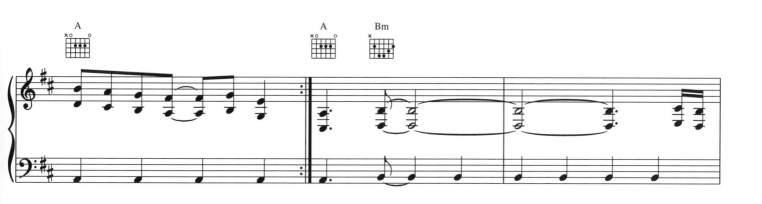

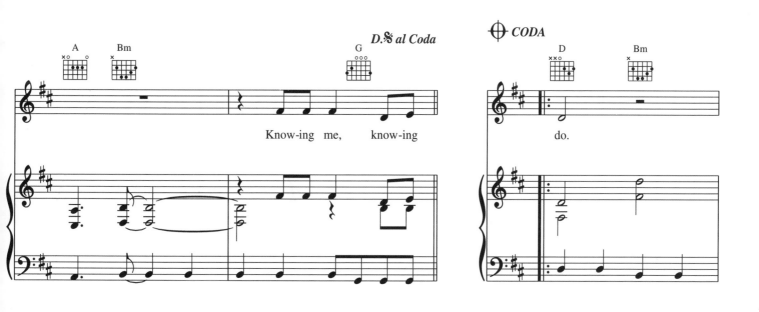

Know-ing me, know-ing

D.%al Coda

⊕ *CODA*

do.

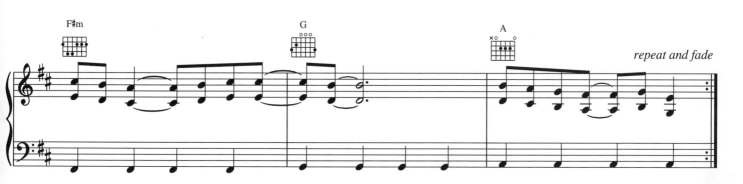

repeat and fade

LAY ALL YOUR LOVE ON ME

WORDS & MUSIC BY BENNY ANDERSSON & BJÖRN ULVAEUS

1. I was-n't jea - lous be - fore we met, now ev'-ry wo - man I see is a po -
2. It was like shoot - ing a sit - ting duck, a lit - tle small - talk, a smile and, ba - by,
3. I've had a few lit - tle love af - fairs, they did - n't last ve - ry long and they've been

-ten-tial threat,
I was stuck.
pret-ty scarce.

and I'm po-ses-sive, it is-n't nice,
I still don't know what you've done with me,
I used to think that was sen-si-ble,

you've heard me say-ing that smok-ing was my on-ly vice.
a grown-up wo-man should nev-er fall so ea-si-ly.
it makes the truth ev-en more in-com-pre-hen-si-ble.

But
I
'Cause

now it is-n't true,__
fell a kind of fear__
ev'-ry-thing is new,__

now ev'-ry-thing is new__
when I don't have you near,__
and ev'-ry-thing is you,__

and
un-
and

43

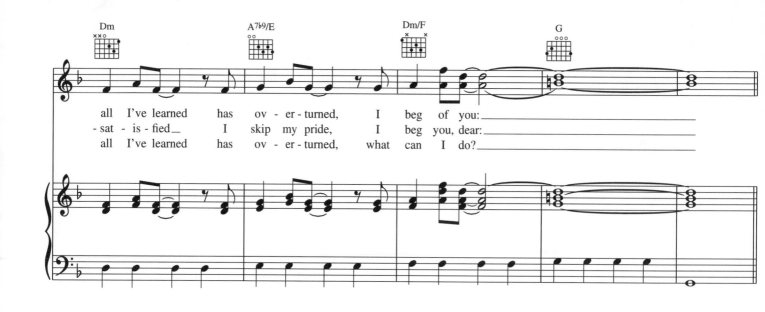

all I've learned has ov - er - turned, I beg of you:___
- sat - is - fied__ I skip my pride, I beg you, dear:___
all I've learned has ov - er - turned, what can I do?___

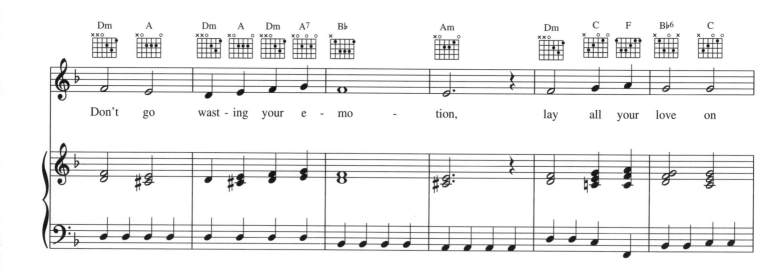

Don't go wast - ing your e - mo - tion, lay all your love on

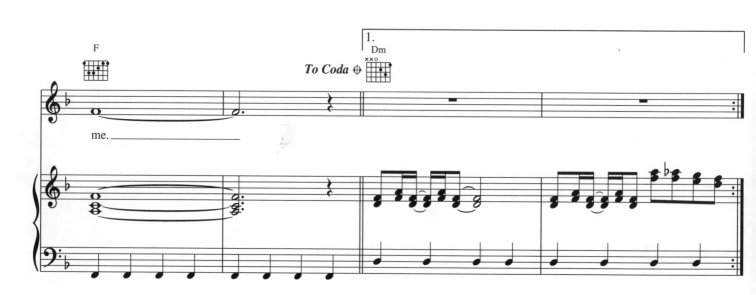

me.___

1.

To Coda

45

MONEY, MONEY, MONEY

WORDS & MUSIC BY BENNY ANDERSSON & BJÖRN ULVAEUS

Steady four

1. I

work all night, I work all day to pay the bills I have to pay.___
man like that is hard to find, but I can't get him off my mind.___

Ain't it sad,_____
Ain't it sad,_____

and
and

still there ne - ver seems to be a sin - gle pen - ny left for me,_____
if he ha - pens to be free I bet he would - n't fan - cy me,_____

that's too bad._____
that's too bad._____ So

In my dreams_____ I have a plan,_____
I must leave,_____ I'll have to go_____

if I got me a weal - thy man_____ I
to Las Ve - gas or Mo - na - co,_____ and

ONE OF US

WORDS & MUSIC BY BENNY ANDERSSON & BJÖRN ULVAEUS

1. They passed me by,—— all of those great ro - man - ces.
(Verse 2 see block lyric)

You were, I felt, rob-bing me—— of my right - ful chan - ces.

My pic - ture clear,— ev - 'ry-thing seemed so ea - sy,——— and so I

dealt you the blow,— one of us had to go.—— Now it's diff-'rent I want you to know.

One of us is cry-in', one of us— is ly-in' in her lone-ly

bed. Star-ing at the ceil-ing, wish-ing she was some-where else— in-

-stead._____ One of us is lone-ly, one of us— is

on-ly wait-ing for a call.__ Sor-ry for her

Verse 2:
I saw myself as a concealed attraction
I felt you kept me away from the heat of the action
Just like a child, stubborn and misconceiving
That's how I started the show one of us had to go
Now I've changed and I want you to know.

One of us is cryin' *etc.*

OUR LAST SUMMER

WORDS & MUSIC BY BENNY ANDERSSON & BJÖRN ULVAEUS

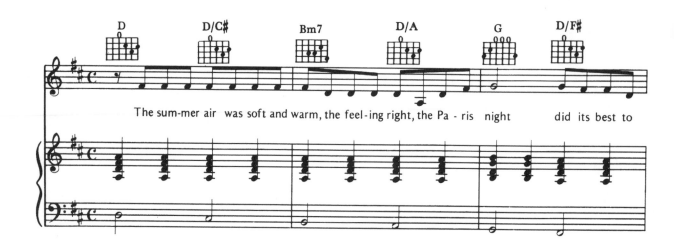

The sum-mer air was soft and warm, the feel-ing right, the Pa - ris night did its best to

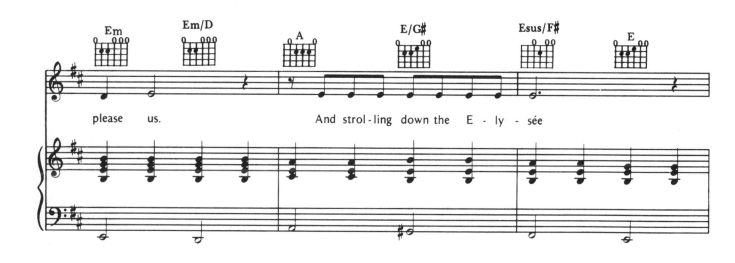

please us. And strol-ling down the E - ly - sée

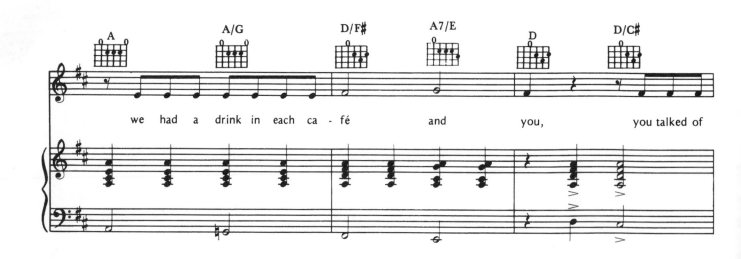

we had a drink in each ca - fé and you, you talked of

rain, our last sum - mer, mem'-ries that re - main.
Dame, our last sum - mer, walk - ing hand in

We made our way a - long the riv - er and we sat down in the grass by the Eif - fel

Tow - er, ___ I was so hap - py we had met,

it was the age of no re - gret, oh yes.

-rants, our last sum - mer, mor-ning cro-is-sants, _____ liv - ing for the

day, wor-ries far a - way, our last sum - mer, we could laugh and play.

(git. solo ad lib.)

D.S., repeat chorus ad lib. and fade

SLIPPING THROUGH MY FINGERS

WORDS & MUSIC BY BENNY ANDERSSON & BJÖRN ULVAEUS

1. School bag in hand,— she leaves home in the ear - ly morn - ing
(Verse 2 see block lyric)

wav - ing good - bye with an ab - sent - mind - ed smile.

I watch her go—— with a surge of that

well known sad - ness,   and I have to sit____ down____ for a while.____

The feel - ing_____ that I'm loos-ing her____ for - ev - er

and with-out real - ly en - ter - ing her world.____

I'm glad when - ev - er I____ can share her laugh - ter, that

63

funny little girl.____ Slip-ping through my

fin-gers all the time,____ I try to cap-ture ev-'ry min-ute,____
(Instr. on D.%.)

the feel-ing in____ it. Slip-ping through my fin-gers all the time,____ do I real-ly

see what's in her mind?____ Each time I think____ I'm close to know-ing____

Verse 2:

Sleep in our eyes, her and me at the breakfast table
Barely awake I let precious time go by.
Then when she's gone there's that odd melancholy feeling
And a sense of guilt I can't deny.
What happened to the wonderful adventures,
The places I had planned for us to go?
Well, some of it we did but most we didn't
And why, I just don't know.

Slipping through my fingers *etc.*

SUPER TROUPER

WORDS & MUSIC BY BENNY ANDERSSON & BJÖRN ULVAEUS

Su- per Trou- per beams are gon- na blind___ me but I won't feel

blue like I al- ways do,___ 'cause some- where in the crowd there's

you.

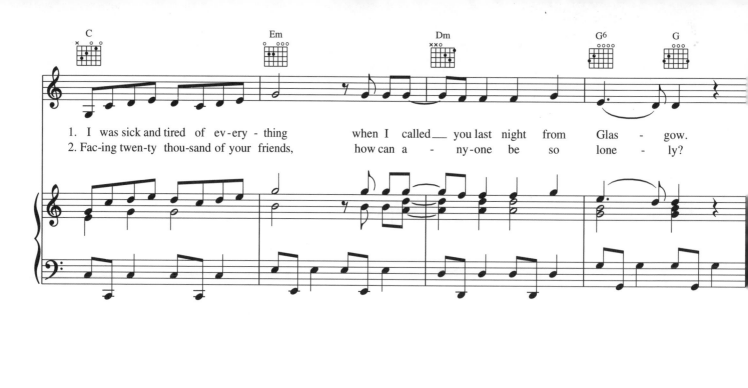

1. I was sick and tired of ev-ery - thing   when I called___ you last night from Glas - gow.
2. Fac-ing twen-ty thou-sand of your friends,   how can a - ny-one be so lone - ly?

All I do is eat and sleep and sing,   wish-ing ev - ery show was the last_____ show.
Part of a suc-cess that nev - er ends,   still I'm think - ing a - bout you on - ly.

So i - ma - gine I was   glad to hear you're com-ing,___   sud-den-ly I feel al - right,
There are mo-ments when I   think I'm go - ing cra-zy,___   but it's gon-na be al - right,

and it's gon-na be so dif-ferent when I'm on the stage to - night._____ To-night the
ev-ery-thing will be so dif-ferent when I'm on the stage to - night._____

Su - per Trou - per lights are gon-na find__ me, shin - ing like the

sun, smil - ing, hav - ing fun,

feel-ing like a num - ber one. To-night the Su - per Trou - per

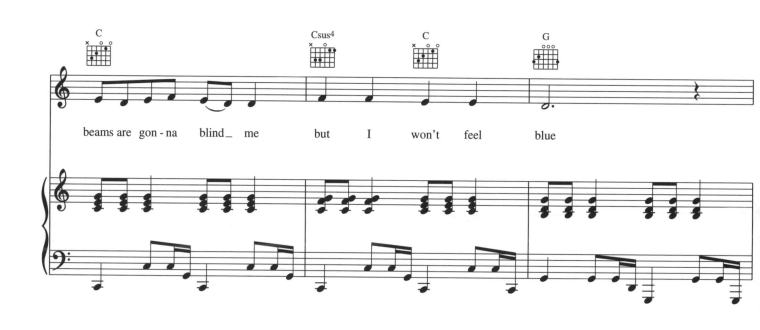

beams are gon - na blind__ me but I won't feel blue

like I al - ways do, 'cause some-where in the crowd there's

S.O.S.

WORDS & MUSIC BY BENNY ANDERSSON, BJÖRN ULVAEUS & STIG ANDERSON

Moderate steady four

1. Where are those hap - py days,___ they seem so hard___ to find?___
2. You seem so far___ a - way,___ though you are stand - ing near.___

I try to reach___ for you,___ but you have closed___ my mind.
You make me feel___ a - live,___ but some - thing died___ I fear.

When you're gone,____ how can I_____ ev - en try__ to go on?_
When you're gone,____ though I try,____ how can I____ car-ry on?_

slower

SUMMER NIGHT CITY

WORDS & MUSIC BY BENNY ANDERSSON & BJÖRN ULVAEUS

Sum-mer night ci-ty,_____

sum-mer night ci-ty._____

Wait-ing for the sun-rise soul - danc-in' in the dark, sum-mer night ci-ty,_____

walk - in' in the moon-light love - mak - in' in a park,

sum - mer night ci - ty._____

In the sun___ I feel___
(Verse 2 see block lyric)

B♭ C Dm

___ like sleep - in' I can't take___ it for___ too long,___

B♭ C

my im - pa - tience slow - ly creep - in' up my spine___ and grow-

79

to sing, _____ in the pale ____ light of ____

_____ the morn - ing no - thing's worth ____ re - mem -

- ber - ing ____ it's a dream, _ it's out ____ of reach ____

scat - tered drift - wood on ____ a beach. _

Wait - ing for the sun - rise soul - - danc - in' in the dark,

sum - mer night ci - ty,_____ walk - in' in the moon - light love -

Repeat to fade

- mak - in' in a park, sum - mer night ci - ty._____

Verse 2:
It's elusive, call it glitter
Somehow something turns me on
Some folks only see the litter
We don't miss 'em when they're gone.
I love the feeling in the air
My kind of people everywhere.
Ah.

When the night comes *etc.*

TAKE A CHANCE ON ME
WORDS & MUSIC BY BENNY ANDERSSON & BJÖRN ULVAEUS

Moderate steady four

If you change your mind__ I'm the first in line,__ ho-ney I'm still free,

take a chance on me,__ if you need me let__ me know, gon-na be a - round

__ if you got no place__ to go when you're feel-ing down. _

If you're all a - lone __ when the pret-ty birds__ have flown, ho-ney I'm still free,

THE NAME OF THE GAME

WORDS & MUSIC BY BENNY ANDERSSON, BJÖRN ULVAEUS & STIG ANDERSON

93

THANK YOU FOR THE MUSIC

WORDS & MUSIC BY BENNY ANDERSSON & BJÖRN ULVAEUS

94

ask in all ho-ne-sty. ____ What would life be ____ with-out a song ____ or dance, ____ what are we? So I say thank-you for the mu-sic, for

1.

giv-ing it to me. ____

To Coda ⊕

2.

I've been so

THE WINNER TAKES IT ALL

WORDS & MUSIC BY BENNY ANDERSSON & BJÖRN ULVAEUS

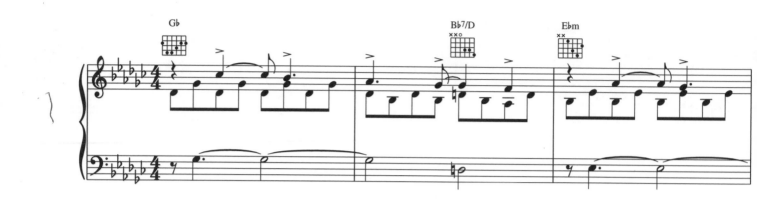

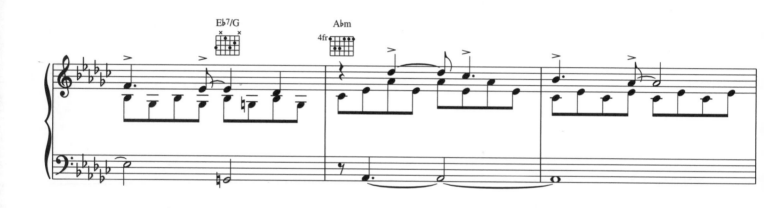

1. I don't wan - na

say,   no more ace   to   play.   The win - ner takes   it
fool,   play - ing   by   the   rules.   The gods may throw   a
say,   rules must be   o - beyed.   The jud - ges will de -
tense,   no self-con - fi - dence.   The win - ner takes   it

all,   the lo - ser stand-ing   small   be - side the vic - to -
dice,   their minds as cold as   ice,   and some-one way down
- cide   the likes of me a - bide,   spec - ta - tors of the

- ry, _____ that's __ her des - ti - ny. _____ 2. I was in your
here _____ lo - ses some-one   dear. _____
show _____ al - ways stay - ing   low. _____

101

The win - ner takes it

all.

repeat and fade

102

UNDER ATTACK
WORDS & MUSIC BY BENNY ANDERSSON & BJÖRN ULVAEUS

1. Don't know how to take it, don't know— where to go,— my re - sis-tance run-ning low,—
(Verse 2 see block lyric)

—— and ev - 'ry day the hold is get - ting tight - er—— and it trou - bles me so.—

—— I'm no - bo - dy's fool and yet it's —— clear to me,—
You know that I'm no - bo - dy's fool.

I don't have a stra - te - gy.—— It's just like tak - ing can - dy from a ba - by,——

Verse 2:
This is getting crazy, I should tell him so
Really let my anger show
Persuade him that the answer to his questions
Is a definite no.
I'm kind of flattered, I suppose.
Guess I'm kind of flattered but I'm scared as well
Something like a magic spell
I hardly dare to think of what would happen
Where I'd be if I fell…

Under attack *etc.*

VOULEZ-VOUS

WORDS & MUSIC BY BENNY ANDERSSON & BJÖRN ULVAEUS

1. Peo-ple ev-ery-where, a sense of ex-pec-ta-tion hang-in' in ___ the air, ___
2. I know what you think, ___ the girl means bus-iness so I'll of-fer her ___ a drink, ___